99 THOUGHTS
FOR STUDENT LEADERS

TAKE RISKS   SERVE OTHERS   LOVE GOD

D0818424

RLIN

simply for students

99 Thoughts for Student Leaders
Take Risks, Serve Others, Love God

© 2012 Doug Franklin

group.com
simplyyouthministry.com

Credits
Author: Doug Franklin
Executive Developer: Nadim Najm
Chief Creative Officer: Joani Schultz
Editor: Rob Cunningham
Cover Art and Production: Veronica Preston

ISBN 978-0-7644-8973-0

10 9 8 7 6 5 4 3 2   20 19 18 17 16 15 14 13

Printed in the United States of America.

TABLE OF CONTENTS

A NOTE FROM THE AUTHOR

As leaders, we're not always going to do things right. We're going to make mistakes. We're even going to make some decisions that lead to failures. We need to learn from those mistakes and continue to take risks. If we really are committed to Jesus Christ, and if we believe that he is the answer for this world, then we'll continue to take risks in his name, not worrying about failure. We will share Christ with people in this world who may never change. We will work at solving problems that seem impossible, and we will care for the least even when it doesn't make sense. This is what leaders do when they are committed to Christ.

Leadership is not a job title. The leaders who make a difference couldn't care less about their position. So someone gave you the title of *student leader*—who cares? If a leader doesn't actually lead, followers won't actually follow. Leaders don't have a title; they have a responsibility that comes from Christ.

This book is about developing your leadership heart. The thoughts and ideas in this book are designed to encourage and to challenge you, to make you think and to help you be creative. This book is not designed to send you into another meeting just to talk about leadership; it's designed to inspire you to lead change. Student leaders are powerful when they follow the call of God, take risks, and challenge other students to follow Christ.

With that in mind, let's get out there and have a few good failures, because that means we're taking risks. Nothing great has ever happened without great risk. So let's fail, learn, and grow as leaders, all for the mission of Christ.

CHAPTER I
STARTING OUT

1: LEADERSHIP CHANGES EVERYTHING

Nothing great has ever happened without a leader. Nothing. Everything meaningful that takes place, that changes lives, that alters the future, can be linked somehow to a leader. It's inescapable. Every well that's built in Africa, every victim rescued from trafficking, every fight for justice is somehow linked to someone's leadership. Whether we want to or not, we all have the power to influence and to be influenced. And we are all drawn to that power when we face situations we want to change. When we are discontent, disappointed, or discouraged, we desire something to change. And from that desire, leadership is often born.

Think of the last time you were discontent. Or the last time you wanted to see change. What did you do about it?

In small and large ways, we all wield the power of leadership in order to make change. We look to get people on our side, to have others see our point of view. Even if it's just getting a teacher to move a test date by lobbying a cause and getting others to support you, you have embarked on leadership. And in the end, any change that is made in the world, in your community, your friends, or your family, will always be linked to someone's leadership.

So what if we knew how to wield this power in a way that upheld and valued those following us? What if we were intentional so that our influence on this world wouldn't be makeshift or happenstance? The kingdom of God desperately needs leaders. It needs radical Christ-followers that will influence the world in a way that shakes it up and reveals a Savior to both the least and the greatest. When Jesus went to heaven, he charged us with a mission that would cost us everything and require us to lead others. He told us to *"Go and make disciples" (Matthew 28:19)*. Making disciples means that we will have to be influencers. We will have to be leaders (great ones) that will show others the road and continue on the greatest mission ever given. Our leadership will change everything.

2: LEADERS ARE WHAT GIVE LEADERSHIP A BAD NAME

It's true, leadership does change everything, but not every change is good. I run into people all over the world who stay as far away from leadership as possible, and I don't blame them. If you watch the news for more than 15 minutes, it's daunting to see how bad leadership can be. It's almost sickening. We learn about people who use the power of leadership for their own personal gain. They take advantage of others, and regularly lead communities and even entire countries into bad circumstances. There are a lot of bad leaders out there. And these bad leaders can give leadership a bad name.

If you are turned off from leadership, ask yourself why. Is it leadership, or is it the bad things you've encountered from bad leaders? Hitler was a leader. He created change, he influenced. And he was bad enough to make anyone want to throw leadership to the sidelines and isolate themselves from being influenced. But Martin Luther King Jr., Nelson

Mandela, William Wilberforce, the Apostle Paul, Jesus Christ, and many others were also leaders. They spread influence that was good, was life-saving, and even overcame the power of bad leaders around them. Leadership itself is not bad, but leaders sure can be.

3: GOOD LEADERSHIP DOESN'T HAPPEN BY ACCIDENT

One of the reasons I wanted to write this book is because I wanted to help good leaders be effective in changing the world. Good leadership does that: It makes change happen. This is one reason why leaders are so important and why we should take leadership seriously. When leaders are unequipped, they can unintentionally be bad change agents, making quick decisions that create more problems than solutions. But when they are prepared and in relationship with Christ, their influence can be unstoppable. Good leadership requires focus, accountability, and a vision of where you are leading others.

Without these things, even good people can be bad leaders.

4: LEADERSHIP ISN'T A POSITION

I think this is the good news about leadership. You might be reading this book because you have been placed in a position of leadership, but don't fall into the trap of believing that your position is what makes you a leader. Titles don't make you a leader, impact does. If you want to be a leader, serve others and improve their lives—and you will be leading. This means you need to focus on growing your leadership skills and growing your character (we'll cover skills and character later on). But here are a few questions that can help you in the process:

1. Do the people you are leading think you value them more than yourself?

2. How well are you listening to your

followers? Do you know what they really need?

3. Do you have a clear understanding of what your position entails as the leader in this team? (In other words, what is your job description and what is expected of you?)

5: LEADERSHIP BALANCES SKILLS AND CHARACTER

It is important for leaders to understand that they must balance skills and character. Getting the job done is just as important as telling the truth. Psalm 78:72 says this: *And David shepherded them with integrity of heart; with skillful hands he led them.* This describes how King David had honesty and how, at the same time, he skillfully led his people. I believe being a great leader involves both leadership skills (what you do as a leader) and character (who you are as a leader). Leaders must always balance these two aspects of leadership. What are you more focused on, doing the job or having character?

6: LEADERSHIP CAN BE LEARNED

Not only do I believe this, I count on it. Today, I am not the leader I was 10 years ago, or even a month ago, and I'm thankful for that. As I pursue Christ and embrace his mission, I am constantly a work in progress. And as I'm faithful and obedient, I find my responsibility and influence growing. I need to be a better leader tomorrow than I am today. If I'm not, I'm doing a disservice to the people who look up to me and who are influenced by me. Even worse, I'm doing a disservice to the kingdom work God has for me.

Regardless of where we start on the leadership journey, we all can learn more as we go. The process of taking risks, communicating well, focusing hard, and casting vision will develop you into a good leader. And in that learning process, you're going to grow as a Christ-follower, too.

7: CHARTING THE COURSE

If you get out a map and figure out how to get from point A to point B, you have charted a course. Deciding how many miles you would go each day, where you would stop for breaks, if you will drive or take a bus, and how long it will take you to get there takes that plan to the next level. Leaders chart the course for their team. Your team may not be literally trying to move from point A to point B, but it may be trying to lead a food drive, plan an event, or organize a vacation Bible school. No matter what, the people on your team need a course to follow and they need a plan. Being able to make the plans that allow your team to reach its goals is an important ingredient to leadership. Leaders make plans and follow through on those plans.

8: MISSION FIRST, PEOPLE ALWAYS

God has given us the mission of making disciples, and God calls us to work with each other to accomplish this mission. So leaders must have an equal value for the mission and for people. Leaders often either value the mission or people, which means they can end up neglecting the one they don't value. But in leadership, mission and people are tied together. Great leaders understand this and work hard to care for people while still reaching their goals. Leaders have a heart that says, "Mission first, people always."

9: UNDERSTANDING YOUR ROLE

Leaders need to understand their role and every aspect of the task at hand. You might even say they need a job description. As a leader you need to know not only what is expected of you, but also where you shouldn't spend your time. Leaders can easily try to lead too much, to take on more than they are able, or to mess with other people's responsibilities. A good job description gives structure and freedom to a leader. If you don't have a job description, ask for one and work through what your responsibilities are and are not.

The more detail you can get, the better it will help you lead.

10: WHAT TO EXPECT

On any team it is important that all members have the same set of expectations about what they are trying to accomplish and how it will be accomplished. It is the job of the leader to set these expectations and make sure they are followed. Healthy expectations create a culture of respect, maintain a spirit of hard work, and build strong community. Healthy expectations are also very clear, detailed yet easily understood, and always upheld. Reviewing expectations regularly with your team is crucial in creating ownership and accomplishing a mission.

Here are some questions to consider about your team's expectations:

1. Does each person know his or her role?

2. Is each person committed to the team?

3. Does each person carry his or her own load?

If you answered no to any of these questions, the people on your team probably don't really understand what's expected of them.

CHAPTER 2
THE HEART OF A LEADER

11: IT ALL COMES DOWN TO YOUR HEART

It's true. Everything in leadership boils down to this one simple thing: If your heart is not OK, the rest of you won't be either. Jesus said it this way in Luke 6:45: *"A good man brings good things out of the good stored up in his heart, and an evil man brings evil things out of the evil stored up in his heart. For the mouth speaks what the heart is full of."* Our words, our actions, and our thoughts all flow from what is inside the heart. If our heart is corrupt, our lives are as well. So the question becomes: How's your heart?

12: SEE THE NEEDS OF OTHERS

Christ-like leaders see the world in a different way. We've all encountered these types of people. They jump at every opportunity to serve others, asking questions such as: "How can I help?" "Is there anything I can do?" "Do you need a hand with that?" These leaders are not focused on themselves. They walk around with eyes wide-open, looking for opportunities to serve others. True leaders understand that they have been given great skills and abilities, and that serving others brings glory to God. As a leader, do you see others as a way to help yourself, or do you look at others and wonder, "How can I help?" The answer reveals a lot about your heart.

13: CONNECT WITH GOD

In leadership, staying connected to God is key. If we lose that connection, we lose our foundation. Knowing our Creator reveals to us more about ourselves, helping us become better leaders. So how do you stay connected to God? Here are just a few ideas:

1. Hang out with people who know God. When you spend more time with others who know God deeply, you learn from them and from their experiences.

2. Read the Bible. It's God writing to you, so it makes sense that in order to stay connected to God, you would read his words.

3. Talk to God. Are you spending time praying to God, speaking your heart to God, and allowing God to speak to you? These three things can help you so much in staying connected to God and following his leadership.

14: SEEK WISDOM

Leadership is hard. Sometimes it throws us curve balls we never saw coming. There are days when we are asked to lead in situations where we have no experience and we feel doomed to fail. God knows this and wants to help us through the challenges we face in leadership. In fact, here's what the book of James tells us: *If any of you lacks wisdom, you should ask God, who gives generously to all without finding fault, and it will be given to you (James 1:5).* God's wisdom is so much better than our own, and it's a freebie! Whether it's the trials or the triumphs of leadership, God desires to see us through it, pouring wisdom into us to help with every decision.

15: FULL OF COMPASSION

Leaders should be compassionate people because we serve a compassionate God. We should be willing to stop everything we have going on in order to show compassion to others around us. The Apostle Paul directly addresses this in 2 Corinthians 1:3-7. He describes God as a compassionate father who comforts us in our time of need so that we can comfort others who are going through hard times. Compassion isn't always easy, though. It will always cost something. Whether it's our time or our resources, we will always give of ourselves. Yet as we show others compassion, we actually reflect God and allow others to see God. Whatever that costs us, it's worth it.

16: LOVE OTHERS MORE THAN YOURSELF

Have you ever been around leaders who only care about themselves, or people who only really want to hang out if you are doing something they enjoy? Or maybe they only give their time and service to things that are all about them, to causes they care about, or to things that benefit their own lives. To be honest, who wants to follow people who only care about themselves? That isn't leadership. Authentic leaders care about others more than they care about themselves, and they use their lives to show it. They build others up and take the opportunity to brag about their team rather than bragging about themselves. Real leaders serve others whenever they get the chance and always put others first.

17: SACRIFICE

Being a leader requires living a sacrificial life. To truly care for others around you, you must be willing to sacrifice for them. Without sacrifice, your followers won't really know how much you care about them. Sacrifice is easy to talk about but hard to do. In order to sacrifice, you must be willing to take less than you deserve, serve others around you, and give more than you think you can. Jesus once told his own followers, *"Greater love has no one than this: to lay down one's life for one's friends"* (John 15:13). Truly caring for our friends and followers requires sacrifice. What are you willing to give?

18: LOVE CONSISTENTLY

We all play favorites, right? And it's not that big of a deal, right? Wrong—it's incredibly damaging! The truth is that as leaders, one of the hardest things for us to do is avoid showing favoritism. The book of James is very clear on God's view toward favoritism: *My brothers and sisters, believers in our glorious Lord Jesus Christ must not show favoritism (James 2:1).* James goes on to tell his readers that people who show favoritism are like judges with evil thoughts. They look only at the outside of a person and never at the heart. When we as leaders play favorites, it communicates a lack of value to our followers and can totally destroy trust.

19: LEADERS ARE RELATIONAL

Leaders aren't just taskmasters who drive an agenda and meet goals. Leaders know that people matter and relationships are important. Leaders must have high relational intelligence, meaning they need to know what is going on between them and their followers, and among their followers. They are quick to identify conflict and unresolved issues. Leaders know when things aren't right relationally, and they work to fix it. Leaders also need to care for their followers and know their greatest needs, hurts, and desires. Relationships matter to leaders.

20: LEADERS GET THINGS DONE

It's not enough for leaders to just be good at building relationships, caring for team members, and making sure people are ready to work together. They must also be about setting goals and making sure they get things done. It's great if the people on your team really like each other and get along, but if they did nothing and never pursued a mission, they were really no different than another group of friends. Leaders must be able to move their entire team down the mission road and do things that really matter.

CHAPTER 3
WHAT LEADERS DO

21: LEADERSHIP IS MORE THAN BEING RESPONSIBLE

A lot of times, people confuse being responsible and being a leader. Being a leader means so much more than just being responsible for things. Leaders do more than just show up on time, meet expectations, and appear reliable to others. Leaders come early and stay late, leaders exceed expectations, and leaders call others to the same standards they live by. Leadership is more than just being good, more than just being nice, more than just being responsible. God-honoring leaders have a big vision to see the world transformed for Jesus Christ. They see areas where they have influence, and they make a difference there. Yes, leaders are responsible, reliable, and trustworthy, but they are so much more than just that.

5 TASKS OF A LEADER

22: TASK 1—DETERMINE THE SCOPE AND GOALS

The next five thoughts are simply five things that leaders must do for every project or mission they face. I always go to these first when I'm faced with a new leadership challenge.

The first task is to determine the scope and goals. One of the greatest challenges of being a leader is envisioning the future. Leaders must be able to set the boundaries of a project and determine goals to ensure the project will be completed with excellence. To do this effectively, you need vision. Vision helps you see ahead of your followers so you can successfully chart the course for them. By determining the scope and goals for the project, it will help your followers know exactly what needs to be accomplished.

23: TASK 2—CALCULATE THE PEOPLE AND RESOURCES

The second task is being able to calculate the people and resources needed to accomplish the task. As a leader you need to put the right people into the right positions so the team can perform at its highest potential. People bring hands to do the work, ideas to do things more effectively, and experience to overcome problems that arise. As a leader you also need to equip your team with the proper resources to complete projects. These resources may include money, materials, or any other necessities. You'll be spared a lot of headaches down the road if you calculate the people and resources well.

24: TASK 3—CAST VISION

The third task is casting the vision. Remember the vision that emerged while you were determining the scope and goals of the project? Well, now it's time to communicate that vision to your followers. A clearly communicated vision can change everything. If you are able to articulate the vision, obstacles won't stand in the way of your mission. However, don't assume that you can get away with just casting the vision once, thinking it will be enough to inspire your followers on the long road of completing your project. No, you need to cast the vision to others continually, reminding them of why they are doing what they are doing. People need constant reminders. Make sure you constantly cast the vision.

25: TASK 4 — NAVIGATE THE OBSTACLES

The fourth task is navigating obstacles. As a leader you need to think constantly about what is coming next, attempting to deal with problems before those issues sabotage a project. Navigating obstacles is different from problem solving, however. Problem solving is dealing with a problem as it arises, while navigating obstacles is looking ahead, seeing what problems might come, and maneuvering around those problems before they cause an issue for your project. Navigating obstacles takes a lot of thought and a commitment to solving problems that could derail your team.

26: TASK 5 — EVALUATE

The fifth and final task that leaders need to do is evaluate. As a leader you need to ask, "What did we do well?" and "How can we do it better next time?" Consistent, honest evaluation is your tool to bring about growth in followers and to ensure excellence in all that your team does. While evaluation is needed, it often doesn't happen because it is hard. It takes a gut-level honesty that is not always present. Yet if you never stop to see where you are, how do you know where you could be? Evaluation is the key to making sure that the success you had in your project will continue for the next time—and that the failures you had will be avoided. Also remember that celebration is a key part of evaluation. When your team does a good job, don't forget to celebrate!

27: READ YOUR FOLLOWERS

Have you ever been around leaders who work their teams into the ground? These leaders don't often keep their followers for very long. People grow tired of working for a leader who cares very little for them. As leaders we need to constantly know where our followers stand. Are they exhausted from the work we have given them? Are they hurting in their personal life and need someone to listen? If we can't read our followers, we will lose them. When you read your followers well and respond with the correct form of care, you'll cultivate their trust in you and their devotion to you.

28: LIVE IN AN UPSIDE-DOWN TRIANGLE

I think most of us go through our daily lives living in a triangle. Imagine a triangle that's sliced into three separate layers. On the bottom of a triangle is the foundation, the widest part. This part gets most of our time, our energy, our thoughts. I think most of us use this part, the largest part of our life, to think only about ourselves. The second level up is the time we put into others. It's not as much as we pour into ourselves, but it's still a pretty good chunk. Finally we make it to the top level, and for us Christ-followers, this is the time we give to God. It's sad, but it's true.

But Jesus taught a totally different way of living life. He said, " 'Love the Lord your God with all your heart and with all your soul and with all your mind.' This is the first and greatest commandment. And the second is like it: 'Love your neighbor as yourself' " (Matthew 22:37-39). What if we lived our lives like this, in an upside-down triangle? What if we gave Christ the biggest chunk of our lives? Life would sure look a lot different and a whole lot more meaningful.

29: LEAD IN YOUR STRENGTHS

I go on at least a couple of mission trips every year. Most teams that I end up leading bring along someone who is very talented at leading worship. They play the guitar like nobody's business and have an amazing voice that creates an awesome atmosphere for worship. There have been many times that I have sat in those worship circles and wished I could play the guitar—let alone sing—like those worship leaders so I could also bring people before the throne of God in the same way. But I can't. I don't have a musical bone in my body. My fingers don't work like that, and my voice is less than pretty. And that's OK. In fact it's great. God has made me a certain way and has put entirely different strengths into me. When I lead in my strengths, I experience joy. When I try to be someone I'm not, I experience frustration. God has created the church as a body of Christ-followers who all contribute their specific strengths and talents. When we focus on what we are great at, we live as God intended us to live.

30: SET GOALS

As I travel around the country and talk with students, the one thing that continually amazes me is that few students are big dreamers. Students today are worried about making mistakes. They are so focused on doing things right that they are unwilling to take a risk. But I want you to be a big dreamer. And to be a big dreamer, you need to have goals. Goals are essential for you to reach your dreams. Goals only come by focusing on the future. Who you are today is nothing compared to who you will be in the future. But who you are in the future will be determined by which map you follow. Goals are a map to the life that God has always wanted you to have.

31: PUSH FOR MORE

Accomplishing great things does not happen by accident. It requires focus and effort. It also requires a leader who is willing to push his or her team to greatness, to have a focus on winning, to challenge members of a team to become more than who they are. This leader is the type of person who is constantly asking questions such as, "Is there a better way?" These leaders push people on their team (and themselves) to their maximum potential, releasing greatness into the world. When we fail to challenge our teams, we fail to get the best out of our teams. Challenging our teams results in great things taking place.

32: GIVE YOUR TIME

True leaders look at their lives differently. As a leader you can't look at your time as your own. One of the great lies in this world is that our time belongs to us and that we are the masters of our days. This couldn't be further from the truth. As Christ-followers and leaders, our time belongs to our Heavenly Father, and we should live with that truth in mind. Rather than waking up thinking about how to spend each day, look for ways to give your time away to God's purposes. Search for opportunities to give your time to others.

33: GIVE YOUR MONEY

"Do not store up for yourselves treasures on earth, where moths and vermin destroy, and where thieves break in and steal. But store up for yourselves treasures in heaven, where moths and vermin do not destroy, and where thieves do not break in and steal. For where your treasure is, there your heart will be also" (Matthew 6:19-21). These words, taken from Christ's Sermon on the Mount, describe God's view of how we should treat our money. Everything we possess in life—whether talent or treasure—was given to us by God. We need to live with open hands, ready and willing to give as needs arise in the kingdom of God. Christian leadership is not a life of luxury; it is a life marked by generosity.

CHAPTER 4
WHO LEADERS ARE

34: FULL OF CHARACTER

Character is vital in leadership. Without character, leaders think only of themselves and their own needs. Being a person of character rallies others around you because they see a person who emulates the qualities of Christ. Building your character is vital when you are in leadership. Think for a moment about the home you live in. Most of our time is spent in the kitchen, or the living room, or our bedrooms, but are these the most important parts of the house? No, of course not. The most crucial part of any home is the foundation. Without a strong foundation, the entire structure will crumble. Your character is the foundation of who you are. If your character is solid, your leadership will flourish. If your character is faulty, everyone around you will eventually see it, and your leadership will collapse. God calls you to be an example, an influencer, a leader. Without good character, your influence goes nowhere.

35: DON'T BE A JERK

Seriously. Nobody wants to follow a jerk. It's easy for a leader who starts out with the best intentions to end up as a jerk. Many leaders allow their power to go to their head and use it to abuse others or push their own agenda. We've each had a run-in with a leader like this before, and it is never a great experience. Leaders who are (or become) jerks take all the credit from others, thus driving their followers away. Strong, good leaders must be team players. They realize that the people they surround themselves with are their best asset and that they are the ones who actually deserve the credit for accomplishments. Remember: Don't be a jerk. Seriously.

36: BE COMMITTED

Being committed takes a lot of work. It requires that you say what you mean and mean what you say. Disappointment happens all the time. People throw out promises they don't intend to keep. They commit to doing things but then change their minds at the last minute. It happens a lot, but this should never characterize your leadership. Leaders are called to a different standard. They must keep their word at all times. The primary reason for this is trust. People won't follow you if they don't trust you. In the book of James, God calls for our "yes" to mean "yes" and for our "no" to mean "no" (see James 5:12). As leaders, it's vital for us to be true to our commitments. Are you a person who means what you say, or do you waver with each passing day?

37: YOUR INTEGRITY MATTERS

Integrity is the ability to live out core values in an honest and consistent manner in all situations. In any situation, when you violate your integrity, it will cost you something. As a leader, when you violate your integrity, it will cost you everything. How do you measure someone's integrity? The only way we as humans can get a fix on this is by looking at their actions. Your actions reveal your heart. What you believe and think will eventually affect your actions. Living with integrity is never easy, and it will certainly come with its hard days, but always remember that God is calling us every day to be the kind of leaders who stay strong in the face of adversity, keeping our integrity no matter what. It's hard but always worth it in the end.

38: TAKE COURAGE

Courage is what enables us to face danger, fear, or trials with confidence, resolution, and bravery. It is not just the absence of fear in our lives; courage is having the strength, power, and will to be different. Courage means standing up for what you know is right, no matter what the consequences might be. Courageous leaders choose to stand for God's truth despite unusual trials, unfair attacks, and unexpected persecution. Through it all, courage pushes you to remain consistent in your determination to stand for what is right. How do you grow in courage? It begins with

the quality of your personal relationship
with God. Courageous leaders learn to live a
consistent life of constant devotion to God in
all circumstances. The more time you spend
time connected with Christ, the more your
conviction and courage will grow.

39: BEING OBEDIENT

Obedience is the act of carrying out a
command or order. The choice of whether or
not to comply lies solely with the recipient
of the command or order. Most likely you are
used to being told what to do. Your parents
tell you, "Clean up your room." Your teacher
says, "Don't forget to do your homework." The
coach announces, "Run another lap around
the field." Sometimes it seems that commands
are the order of the day! However, the way
you respond to the commands of people in
authority over you says a great deal about your
character. God-honoring obedience occurs
immediately, willingly, and joyfully. Philippians
2:5 encourages us to have the same humble
attitude that Jesus displayed. Christ took his

obedience all the way to the cross, and he did it willingly (v. 8). When we are obedient to God and to the leaders above us, it shows both respect and love. And when we know how to follow well, we understand more fully how to lead well.

40: PERSEVERE

Leadership is hard! Problems will arise, obstacles will occur, and people will disappoint. The true test of leadership is what happens when everything goes wrong. When a "rogue wave" smashes hopes and dreams, persevering leaders stay at the helm and hold on tightly, and either weather the storm or go down with the ship! Perseverance is the steadfast determination to keep on keeping on. The Apostle Paul described perseverance in Philippians 3:13-14: *Forgetting what is behind and straining toward what is ahead, I press on toward the goal to win the prize for which God has called me heavenward in Christ Jesus.* Leadership is hard, but know that for those who persevere through struggles and hardships, a great prize awaits.

41: COMMUNITY IS IMPORTANT

It seems popular these days for people to publicly announce how they want to be followers of Jesus but don't want to be associated with other Christians. Like you could somehow separate the two! A huge part of becoming a follower of Christ is learning how to live in community with other Christ-followers. The church is a community, a group of people who come together to worship, learn, and encourage one another in their faith. When you surround yourself with other Christ-like people, you invite God to work in your life through the body of Christ. These people will challenge you, bring out your gifts, affirm God's work in your life, carry your burdens, and help you grow more than any book or class ever will. As leaders we especially need meaningful relationships with other Christians. No man (or woman) is an island. God didn't design us that way.

CHAPTER 5
LEADERS HAVE TEAMS

42: VALUE TEAMWORK

Teamwork is an obvious essential to every great team. A team that cannot work together is a team that is ineffective. However, to get people to work together and to have amazing teamwork, you must value teamwork itself. Having a value for teamwork is the first aspect of a well-working team. What I mean by this is that each member, and especially the leader, must care deeply about the team and its members. When some members don't care, it affects the entire team. Showing value to your team often comes in the form of believing in others. When you show confidence in your teammates and their abilities, it builds trust and value for the team in all of the members. When you have a team whose members value each other, there isn't much that can stand in your way.

43: LEADERS MUST BE IN THE TRENCHES

Team leaders must be in the trenches with their teams. Even though they may not be present at every team meeting and may give their team freedom to move without them, there still must be a strong sense among team members that the leader is "in this with them." It is important for team leaders to establish a hands-on presence by visiting the team, holding recognition ceremonies, and showing their team's success to other people. A team leader who is too busy to participate or who chooses to invest in other endeavors will not only frustrate their team, but also likely will see the team reap poor results.

44: LEADERS FIGHT FOR THEIR TEAM

One of the most important jobs a team leader can do is to fight for their team. A team leader has or finds access to funds, information, and even simple things such as meeting spaces that other team members can't get. Beyond finding the resources that a team needs, team leaders are key in getting the right people onto their teams. Leaders who find good talent and add vital team members empower their teams.

Team leaders also fight for their team by being a great advocate to authority figures such as a teacher, boss, youth pastor, or manager. They continually give updates to the leaders of their organization on how the team is doing, along with its needs and wins. This helps the team receive support from people on the outside and gain the recognition and rewards it deserves.

45: LEADERS KEEP THE TEAM GOAL IN SIGHT

A leader plays a crucial role in keeping the team's purpose and common goal known among the team. When team members lose sight of their goal and drift off into areas that aren't part of the mission, it's the leader's job to pull them back. Leaders of teams need to communicate regularly to people on the team about why they exist and what work they need to do in order to achieve their goal. Alongside this, leaders need to establish a sense of urgency on the team. One of the roles a team leader plays is keeping team goals compelling and creating a sense of urgency for the team.

46: LEADERS HELP PEOPLE WORK TOGETHER

There are several things a team leader can do to help people work together. Team leaders need to use their voice to encourage everyone on the team. They also need to make sure that no one's left out. It's easy as a leader to get comfortable working with a few people. But this sends the message that only a few people are valued. So it's important to help everyone engage in the team's mission. When this happens, your team will have the best ideas, the most potential, and will be able to overcome any obstacle.

47: LEADERS CARRY THEIR TEAMS

Teams need leaders who are champions. People follow a champion. Student leaders who give their all become champions for their team. When a team is down or can't make it through, leaders rise to inspire and encourage their team. When teams are lost or feeling hopeless, leaders bring hope and direction. Leaders don't step up just to be a champion and take all the glory; they give precisely what is needed so their team can succeed and share in the joy of accomplishment together.

48: DELEGATION

Good leaders communicate what needs to be done and who is responsible for doing it. They provide direction and assistance, if needed, and then they follow up to see how things are progressing. As a leader you must delegate what needs to be done and hold your team accountable for doing it. Your role is to be clear on what people's responsibilities are, help set goals to accomplish the job, and be available to answer questions and overcome obstacles. Make sure team members know they are responsible for figuring out how things get done and for doing it. This is part of developing your teammates as leaders.

49: TEAM UNITY

Teams unify because of shared mission—a common purpose and goal. To build unity you must persuade your team members that they have a God-given purpose, something that God determined before the beginning of time, something God invited them to do. Remember, unity ties to your mission. Be sure you are articulate and passionate when presenting the mission. Create specific goals for projects and people. It's easy to create tasks that need to be accomplished, but we can't forget to create goals for encouraging each other and caring for one another. It's also important for your team to have lots of fun together. Team-building games and initiatives are always a great way at creating a sense of unity on a team.

50: ALWAYS KNOW YOUR TEAM'S GREATEST NEED

In college I had a professor who always seemed to pile on massive amounts of homework at the wrong time. Whenever there was a long weekend, an important sporting event, or a bunch of finals coming up, this professor would consistently assign more work to be done. It was like he was trying to destroy his students, his team. He was a leader who did not understand his team; he did not know their needs. If the goal was for students to learn, grow, and appreciate the subject matter, this particular professor failed miserably. Because he gave us more work, we became angry, unmotivated, and resentful. We certainly grew in our hatred of the course material. The professor was a terrible leader because he didn't know the greatest need of his team. Leaders need to constantly be listening, learning, and watching their team. If you do, you'll quickly learn what the team's greatest need is and you can work to meet it so that the team becomes faster, stronger, more efficient, and more successful.

CHAPTER 6
WHAT LEADERS SAY

51: COMMUNICATE, COMMUNICATE, COMMUNICATE

If there is one thing that will make or break a mission, it's communication. Without communication, nothing gets done. With a little communication, your team will probably start down the road but fall short. With bad communication, your team members may end up working against each other and against you. Communication sets the tone, defines the mission, and melds a team together.

Leaders who communicate well aren't always seen talking up-front (after all, the world does not need more talking heads). In fact, they are more apt to communicate in a way that puts others in the spotlight, encouraging and inspiring their team forward.

Leaders who communicate well use their words, their body language, and their listening skills interchangeably. Instead of communicating about problems, they communicate solutions. Instead of taking credit, they point to their team's hard work.

You won't find a good leader mocking or giving a teammate the cold shoulder, but you will see that person patiently listening and casting the vision.

Words are precious, and leaders know this. They hold the power to create change. If you have a mission to change something in your community or in this world, your success will be determined by how well you can communicate.

52: INTENTIONAL COMMUNICATION

There are so many messages being thrown at you every day that it's easy to see why most of them don't stick. Even by the time you get to school in the morning, you've probably taken in more messages than you can count. Between the radio, your cell phone, billboards, and your parents reminding you to grab your jersey for the game, you've had countless people screaming for your attention. The world is full of people and organizations wanting you to just pay them a couple of seconds (sometimes a couple of hours) of attention. So when you're a leader, remember that your communication is competing with thousands of other messages your followers are taking in. How will you make sure your message stands out? Running over a list of logistics in a meeting will probably not cut it.

Be creative with your communication, and make sure it stands out. Use every opportunity with your team members to intentionally build them up and set the course. Team meetings are not usually where the most communication takes place; it's the small messages along the way that make the difference. Use texts, social media, and even just a walk down the hall to be intentional and to build your team up. Those moments will make all the difference in your leadership.

53: POWERFUL COMMUNICATION

Whenever I think about the power of words, I think of the movie *Braveheart*. There comes a point when the small army of peasant

Scotsmen are lining up on the battlefield to face the massive English army (completely outfitted in armor and professional weaponry). The peasants have gathered but are losing heart and don't believe that they can win. So they begin thinking of what they have to negotiate with, in order to avoid a battle. At that moment, in rides William Wallace, the hero of the peasants. He gives an inspiring speech that rallies the Scotsman and prepares them to fight against impossible odds.

Almost every inspiring movie contains that one scene where the circumstances are bleak, but a leader comes in and uses powerful, inspiring words that lead to a game changer. As a leader, you have the opportunity (and maybe even the responsibility) to use powerful words. If your team is in pursuit of anything worthwhile and meaningful, then you can count on the fact that there will be obstacles to overcome. Using words that inspire your team will be the first step in overcoming the obstacles.

54: GRACE-FILLED WORDS

For the most part, things in leadership don't go as planned. Someone will drop the ball (on purpose or not), you will face some sort of misunderstanding, or there will be something that no one thought about. Part of being a leader is being able to deal with circumstances that don't go as intended. The key ingredient is to communicate grace. There are a lot of opportunities to blame or to pass the buck in a passive-aggressive way. There are unlimited ways we can make our teammates pay for a mistake while still keeping a smile on our face, but in the end, it will get you nowhere. Be a leader that offers grace. Stay away from gossip or words that carry the undertones of accusation. Be quick to move forward after a mistake. Don't bring up past offenses, and get used to offering forgiveness. After all, you'll probably need it at some point.

My dear brothers and sisters, take note of this: Everyone should be quick to listen,

slow to speak and slow to become angry,
because human anger does not produce
the righteousness that God desires
(James 1:19-20).

55: REAL ENCOURAGEMENT

We often overlook the power of encouraging words: A note, an intentional compliment, and a meaningful conversation are all ways that a leader can support their followers. We as leaders often get focused on the goal at hand and forget to care for our followers through encouragement. However, followers are so vital to the mission that we must learn to use the power of encouraging words to keep our followers motivated.

As a leader, set the tone for your group by constantly using encouraging words. Many teams are completely void of encouragement, and some can barely get past the occasional "good job." Be the kind of leader who is easy to follow by offering words of encouragement. Start with a simple "thank you" when someone completes a task, and move on to intentional encouragement that shows your teammates how God is working in their lives.

56: DON'T STEAL THE SPOTLIGHT

Have you ever been around people who always talk about themselves? They like to tell you how great they are at sports, or how great they did in their audition for the school play. Sometimes they even tell you how great they are because they read the Bible every day or pray a ton. I call these people conversation hijackers. They swing in and try to one-up your story and make it all about them.

Leaders are focused on others, not themselves. They ask questions (which is a rare gift at any age) that allow others to do the talking, and they listen well. Leaders that do this will find that they can lead their followers anywhere. They will build so much trust and value, that when the time comes to really ask of them, the followers will willingly sacrifice for the leader because of the genuine care that's been displayed.

57: HARD TRUTH

Sometimes good enough isn't actually good enough. If you're really going to effect change in this world, it will cost you and your team something. One of the things leaders must always be willing to do is speak the hard truth. This isn't a call to be a downer or to rail on your team members when they lack focus; it's simply being honest about what it will take to make it. Jesus was great at this. As he led his disciples, he didn't shy away from hard truth. In the Gospel of Luke, Jesus said, *"Whoever wants to be my disciple must deny themselves and take up their cross daily and follow me"* *(Luke 9:23).* Jesus was forthright and bold. It's not a great sales pitch to tell your followers that they're going to have to deny themselves and carry a cross in order to follow him. But it was the truth. Was Jesus loving? Yes. Compassionate? Definitely. Kind? Of course. And did he speak the hard, honest truth? Always.

58: LEADERS ARE CONCISE

Don't bog your followers down by talking in circles and repeating things. Be concise.

59: SELL THE MISSION

This sounds terrible, doesn't it? The idea of "selling" the mission. I can't help but think of a used car salesman, but that's not really what I'm talking about here. What I mean is that leaders often take for granted how much time they spend focused on the project or team they are leading. When you're a leader, you have to be an owner, and therefore what you're leading is constantly on your mind. Your teammates or followers have other things at the forefront of their minds, because they aren't the ones ultimately responsible for the mission. So whenever you meet or work on a project together, remember that you have to put the mission back in the front. You need to take a minute to cast the vision, to tell your team members why they are there and why it's important. Never assume that your team is just as concerned or all in as you are (it's possible, but rare). Take the time to sell the mission.

60: THE MOMENT OF RECOGNITION

At some point in time, you are going to receive recognition for your leadership. You will be told what a great job you did in leading your team or accomplishing something. When this point in time comes, shift the credit back to the people on your team—*their* hard work, *their* dedication, and *their* focus. Truth is, it wasn't all you. You needed them, but they aren't likely to be called out and recognized because none of them is the official "leader." Leaders who give the credit to the team are hard to find and easy to follow.

61: LEADERS POINT OTHERS TO GOD

Leadership doesn't matter unless it carries a kingdom weight. It really doesn't. Ultimately, life comes down to one thing: HIM. Jesus gave us the mission of making disciples.

It requires that we love HIM first, with everything, and that we bring others along with us. At the end of the day, our leadership doesn't matter unless it bears this kingdom weight. Regardless of what your project is, how are you pointing others to God? How are you pointing your followers, the people you serve, and your peers to the ONE who holds everything? Be careful to never think you are so important that your leadership stops pointing others to HIM.

62: LEADERS SAY, "I'M SORRY"

Probably the most powerful phrase you can say as a leader is, "I'm sorry." It's easy to beat around the bush and give excuses, say you did the best you could, or promise to try to do it differently next time. But what your followers need to hear is that you're sorry when things go wrong. It tells them you're human, you're humble, and you're real. It lets them know that you care about them and that you aren't too stuck on yourself to be able to apologize. If you are really leading, you're going to be saying, "I'm sorry" a lot because you're taking risks and learning. But if you struggle with those words, you have a lot more leadership problems than you think, and probably a pride problem. Always be willing to own mistakes, apologize, and practice humility.

CHAPTER 7
WHAT LEADERS NEED

63: LEADERSHIP IS BIGGER THAN YOU

Often as leaders we get a big head. We can allow our position of leadership to determine our value rather than what we actually contribute to the team. Newsflash! Leadership is way bigger than just you. There are always more people involved, more responsibilities than you can handle alone, and more problems than you know how to solve. While you may have been put into a leadership position because of your talents or natural abilities, you have to understand that you'll need certain things for your success to continue. From a deeper knowledge of how you are wired, to wisdom from older leaders who have gone before you, you'll need certain abilities and help from others if you truly are a good leader.

64: DO YOU KNOW WHO YOU ARE?

Have you ever seen someone attempt something they were not equipped for? What happened? Most likely that person failed or at least struggled immensely. Strong leaders know what they are good at and what they aren't. They spend the majority of their time doing the things they are good at because they understand that it will be the best way to help the team. Strong leaders also find support for the areas in which they are weak. Having weaknesses does not make you a weak leader; failing to admit your weaknesses and not finding help makes you a weak leader. Knowing who you are and what you're good at is a huge need in leadership.

Take a moment to consider these questions:

1. What are your areas of strength? If you aren't sure, how can you discover them?

2. What are your weaknesses? If you don't know them, how can you learn what they are?

65: FIND A MENTOR

Life is a journey, a road we all travel. It's how God designed it. But God didn't intend for us to walk the road alone. Rather, God tells us to surround ourselves with people who will come alongside us, provide direction and wisdom, encourage us to stay on course, and challenge us to push ourselves. Jesus did all this as he mentored his disciples, and he wants the same thing for us. As leaders, we each need to find a mentor—someone who comes alongside us on our journey through life. Usually a mentor is someone a little older than you, someone who has more life experience, and someone you trust and respect. That person's experience, combined with your potential, results in a relationship that can lead to transformation.

66: ACCOUNTABILITY

Leadership can oftentimes come with a great deal of power, which can be a good thing, but also a very dangerous thing. Because of this power, it is really easy to become one of those leaders that put themselves on a pedestal—the kind of leaders that look down on others around them. I know that your first reaction is to say, "That will never be me," but there's a reason so many leaders struggle with this. It's a temptation that comes with the territory. This is why accountability is crucial for leaders. When we have someone in our lives who regularly holds us accountable, who asks us challenging questions, and who we are gut-level honest with, it keeps us grounded. Having accountability in our lives keeps us on the same level as others around us, never letting the power that comes with leadership put us on a pedestal. If you don't have someone like this in your life, you need it.

67: FOCUS PRECEDES SUCCESS

One discipline that separates average leaders from great leaders is focus. Leaders who are truly effective can maintain a single-minded focus on the task at hand. Unfortunately, not many leaders out there are able to do this well. Most people struggle to focus at the very time when it is needed most. Think about basketball players. When they shoot a free throw, the thing they need most is focus. That's why opposing fans do everything they can to distract them. The same is true in our lives. When focus suffers, the performance of the team suffers. One of the best ways to strengthen your leadership is to learn how to improve your focus. If you improve your focus and help others around you improve their focus, you'll see incredible results.

Take a moment to consider these questions:

1. When are the vital times that you need to focus as a leader?

2. When are the times your team really needs to focus?

68: A MISSION FOR YOUR LIFE

Leaders need a mission, a goal to urge their followers toward. If leaders have no ultimate goal, no dream of what they can accomplish, they have nothing to lead people toward. Consequently, they end up becoming the blind leading the blind. Every leader has the ability to discover the mission God is calling them to; they just need to be open to what God has been doing in their life. God has crafted you to be the person that you are. God has placed burdens on your heart, has given you passion, and is giving you a vision for what you can accomplish. When you take the time to figure out what these three things are in your life and leadership, it can pave the way for discovering your mission.

Take a moment to consider these questions:

1. What burdens you?

2. What are you passionate about?

3. What God-given dreams do you have for the future?

69: LEAD WITH CONFIDENCE

People with confidence can do amazing things. Often leaders are faced with challenges and don't know what to do, but one of the true tests of leadership is what you do when

you don't know what to do. Leading with
confidence through uncertainty enables
members of a team to trust their leader.
You need to understand, though, that true
confidence comes from a deep understanding
of God in your life. Keep in mind that it will
never be easy to grow in confidence. God will
push you to take risks, to reach outside of your
comfort zone, to do things you would normally
shy away from—but take courage! God is
with you the whole way. As you take risks, as
you step out and lead in uncertain times and
situations, your confidence will grow. And as
your confidence grows, so will your influence.

70: KNOW YOUR TEAM

Every person on your team is different and
unique, just like every person in the world is
different and unique. Every member of your
team has a special contribution to make,
but if you don't know their unique gifts and
abilities, they'll never be able to give as fully
as they can. In 1 Corinthians 12, the Apostle
Paul describes the body of Christ as being

similar to a human body: full of many different parts, each one contributing to help the body function at its greatest capacity. When we know and understand the people who are on our team and place them in the right spots based on their gifts and abilities, our team can accomplish a ton. Ask yourself how well you know your team.

Take a moment to consider these questions:

1. Is anyone in the wrong role based on his or her gifts?

2. Is anyone in the perfect spot?

71: MANAGE YOUR TIME

You need to be better at managing your time. Seriously. When you step back and look at the grand scheme of your life, you need to know that you are going to live forever; the first 70 years or so are going to be here on earth. Do you want to spend your time pursuing kingdom-building activities, or just wasting your days on frivolous things? It's the small stuff that eats up your time. Learn to prioritize. Keep a calendar. Stop watching television so much or playing so many video games. The better you get at managing your time and putting your efforts into things that are worth your time, the more God will trust you. With more trust comes greater influence.

72: YOU NEED FOLLOWERS

If you're a leader, but you don't have anyone following you, are you really a leader? No. You're just going for a walk. So how do you gain and maintain your followers? You need to communicate well. How can a leader call people alongside them to accomplish the mission if the followers have no idea where the leader is going? They can't. It just won't happen. Followers need to know where the leader is going and why they would want to follow. To maintain your followers once you've gained them, you need to care for them wholeheartedly. A huge pitfall of many leaders is that they forget this, and it destroys the loyalty of the people following them. When you communicate with your followers and then care for them, you'll lead them well.

CHAPTER 8
DREAMING LIKE A LEADER

73: LEADERS HAVE A HIGHER PERSPECTIVE

Leaders dream big. Just like you, leaders are
ordinary people who believe that God can do
the extraordinary. They ask God to help them
see the world the way it someday should be—
and could be. With this higher perspective
in place, leaders right wrongs, meet needs,
solve problems, and make possibilities
realities. They mobilize followers, galvanize
commitment, and roll up their sleeves to
take action. Despite hardships and obstacles,
leaders "keep on keeping on" until they fulfill
the dream. But it all starts with the dream,
with the higher perspective that only comes
from faith in God. Faith pushes them to dream
the impossible, and faith is what helps them
fulfill the dream.

74: KNOW YOUR IDENTITY

As a leader in God's kingdom, you need to
know your true identity. You are a child of
God, a child of the king. God created you
uniquely, as someone who is different from

everyone else around you. God has hardwired your DNA with specific skills and talents, and has gifted you through the Holy Spirit to do some pretty amazing things. In order to dream like a leader, you need to know who you are. It can be frustrating and disillusioning to dream about serving God in a specific area if that area isn't where you were wired to serve. But when you know who you are and how you're wired, and you dream within that context, the possibilities of what you can do for God is limitless.

75: SEE POTENTIAL

When you look at others, do you see their problems, or do you see their potential? As leaders we need to see people the way God sees them: as individuals who can accomplish great things. Just as you have been gifted, others around you are gifted as well. It's important to see past your followers' imperfections and give them grace, while helping them dream about who they can grow to be. Your followers may not think they are capable of anything great, and you may be the first person who has ever believed in them. When you see the potential in others rather than just their problems, it allows for greatness to take place.

76: HAVE A CAN-DO ATTITUDE

The power of a positive attitude can't even be measured. It is literally one of the most important things you can maintain as a leader. A can-do attitude inspires your followers, lifting their morale, and it even inspires others outside of your team as well. Even if you say all the right things, if your attitude isn't in the right place, your team will read between the lines. Life is hard, but when we lead with a positive attitude, it makes the hardships we face easier to swallow. The Christian writer Chuck Swindoll once said, "I am convinced that life is 10 percent what happens to me and 90 percent how I react to it." He's right. Our attitude affects everything, for the good and the bad.

77: FOCUS ON THE END—EVEN AT THE BEGINNING

Every person who has ever won a race had one thing in common: They focused the entire time on the finish line. I know this because it is almost impossible to win a race unless you keep the finish line in your sights. As a leader, you must be the one who keeps everyone's focus on the finish line, continually reminding people of what they are working toward. Here's what the Apostle Paul told the Christians in the Greek city of Corinth: *Do you not know that in a race all the runners run, but only one gets the prize? Run in such a way as to get the prize (1 Corinthians 9:24).* The only way we achieve success in leadership is by keeping our focus on the finish line, even if we just stepped over the starting line.

78: BE A RISK TAKER

What's the last risk you took? I mean a real risk, one that stretched you and took you outside of your comfort zone. Sometimes it's hard for us to remember the risks we take because, to be honest, we don't really take that many risks. We live in such a safety-driven society that the thought of stepping out in faith, not knowing if we will fail or succeed, scares most of us into living a life void of risks. And when we live without risks, we also live without adventure, excitement, and dependence on God. As leaders we need to examine our lives and strive to live outside of our comfort zones, continually challenging ourselves and others around us to take risks for Christ. For when we walk in faith, we walk with God.

79: KINGDOM IMPACT

Christianity is a grassroots movement. One person tells another person about their new life in Christ. They share how Christ has redeemed them, forgiven their sins, and brought them into new life. This movement is led by leaders who take risks. Sometimes we share our faith and people reject us. And sometime they accept the truth. Those odds scare us. But leaders realize that the grassroots movement goes forward because of the risks that they take. So they share their life, moving past the fear and demonstrating courage. Whether you're in class, on the athletic field, or at your part-time job, every relationship that you make is a chance to impact the kingdom. The desired result of all leadership is kingdom impact.

CHAPTER 9
LEADING YOUR FRIENDS

80: HONEST TALK

Leading your friends is probably one of the hardest parts of leadership. It seems like it should be the easiest, since your friends already have a positive connection with you, but in reality, that's what makes it so hard. With friends, leaders tend to undercommunicate, because they assume their friends understand them better than others. Leaders also tend to take advantage of friends, knowing that they'll most likely receive grace.

On the flip side, friends can struggle to be led by you. Friendships take place on a level playing field, where no one has more power than the other and everyone's decisions are given equal weight. It's a hard adjustment for a friend to honor your decision when it's in the team's best interest but not necessarily in theirs. It can also be easy for friends to take shortcuts and not pull their weight because they know you'll go easy on them.

Ultimately, the key to leading friends and overcoming all the obstacles is talking honestly from the start. Before you face any of these scenarios, have a conversation with your friends to address these downsides. Let them know that you'll commit to being honest with them and won't treat them differently than the rest of the team, and ask them for the same in return. Tell them how much their support means to you in this role, and give them your best effort at leading. Last, but not least, don't let your leadership role define the rest of your friendship. Be on equal footing when you are just hanging out.

81: SEEK "OUTSIDE" ADVICE

The first place I go for advice and opinions is my friends. I can trust them, and I know they care about me. But when leading friends, sometimes they aren't the first place I should go for advice. Why? Because it could put them in a position that forces them to take sides.

Here are two situations when you should probably get outside advice:

1. When the team isn't getting along— someone isn't pulling their weight, has a bad attitude, or has a personal issue—your friend is going to have to take your side. And quite honestly, you are going to force your friend to judge the "slacker." Be on the safe side, and talk to a neutral party such as a youth pastor or your small group leader.

2. When it's time to evaluate. If you ask your friend how you're doing as a leader, they are going to slant toward the positive side. This is good, but probably not all that accurate. If you want a real reading on how it's going, ask your friends, but also ask others both inside and outside the team.

When should you get advice from your friends? My suggestion is that if you could talk to anyone on your team about it, then not only is it safe to get your friend's advice, but it's also probably helpful and accurate.

82: DON'T TAKE FRIENDS FOR GRANTED

It's the worst when leaders take their friends for granted. Although a friend will probably show up at midnight to give you last-minute help, that person probably won't follow you for long—especially if they see you prepared, encouraging, and intentional with everyone else on the team. Don't give your friends the short end of the stick; remember to encourage them, communicate with them, and honor their commitment. This way, they'll be your biggest advocates and best teammates.

83: HUMILITY!

Few things end friendship faster than arrogance. Even leaders with the best intentions can fall into the trap of seeing themselves as more important than they should. Nobody likes to hang around this type of person. As a leader, be the lowest person on the totem pole, acknowledging and encouraging others' efforts, achievements, and input. Humble leaders are team players. Many leaders lose friendships in the leadership process because they lose sight of how priceless their friends really are. Do your friends really know how important they are to you?

84: YOU SET THE STANDARD

If you just smile and shake your head when your friend shows up late to a team meeting, you are setting the standard for the whole team. Either they'll all think that it's OK to be late and that the team meetings don't matter all that much, or they'll think you have favorites if everyone except your friends is expected to be on time. Our friends can tend to be lax and follow the rules of our friendship rather than that of the team. They may not carry their weight, or they may even expect a free pass from you. But when we give our friends free passes, we will find ourselves in deep water with everyone else. Be consistent.

Set the standard from the start with everyone, and don't treat your friends any differently. This seems obvious, but it can be hard to confront your friends when they don't pull their weight. Be ready to bring back that honest talk, with loads of encouragement.

85: CONFLICT RESOLUTION

As a leader, you are going to face problems and conflict. Thinking that you can avoid problems and conflict, or hoping that you can, just doesn't work. The best approach is to plan now, so that when it happens, you know how to proceed. Here are some tips for dealing with conflict:

1. Start by listening, not with defensiveness. Get the whole scope of the situation by asking lots of questions.

2. If the conflict is between you and a friend, get a neutral person to talk it through with you. If it's between two team members,

don't pick sides. Always remember that peace lies between two opposing views.

3. Move quickly to common ground. Usually people agree about more than they disagree about. Try to focus on what you (or they) can agree about.

4. Stay focused on the mission. Teams that focus on the mission have fewer conflicts. In most cases, conflict comes from something petty and is easily dispersed when the overall mission or value for the friendship is focused on.

CHAPTER 10
LEADING WHEN YOU'RE NOT IN CHARGE

86: LEADERS NEVER STOP LEADING

Whether you are dubbed the leader or not, the truth is that leaders never really stop leading. Regardless of your position, title, or role, you are always influencing. If you are driving your little brother to school, you are a leader. If you are sitting on the bench of a basketball game, you are a leader. If you are serving up mashed potatoes in the lunch line, you're a leader. Life doesn't take place in a vacuum; it takes place in community and in plain sight. How you live demonstrates to others what's important, what the truth is, and what impact you will have on them.

A friend of mine is the leader of a Christian school. He recently had the opportunity to share Christ with the local mayor and his wife because of how some students from his school acted in a Starbucks®. The mayor was sitting in this Starbucks watching how these students interacted with each other, cared for each other, and talked with the employees. He took note and made a point to encourage my friend on what great people this school had in it. This opened the door for my friend to tell him why these students were so different, what they believed, and how it changes their actions.

These students weren't in charge. They had no standing with the mayor of their city and no official role they were filling. They were just having coffee. But even when you are just having coffee, you are influencing—maybe even for eternity. Leaders never stop leading. So when you aren't the one in charge, what kind of influence are you having?

87: FROM LEADER TO FOLLOWER

It's a hard adjustment to be in the role of following a new leader when you are used to being the leader. Whether it's a new year and you've been reassigned, or you aren't the one in charge of a project, be consistent. If you were the "leader" you would be encouraging, solving problems, displaying a positive attitude, and acting responsibly. So if you aren't the leader, why change? Be a great teammate. Be the kind of person you would want on your team if you were in charge. Encourage the leader. Support that person. And have the integrity to be the same person regardless of your position.

88: TEAM CARE

Every time I watch a group of students pile out of the bus at the beginning of a retreat or mission trip, I can tell how much they really care about each other. I can tell by how they unload the bus. Usually, each person will only touch their own bag, waiting on the side until it becomes available. This kind of team will struggle to make an impact or be unified. They probably won't watch each other's back or take many risks. Most likely they'll play it safe and only think about their individual roles, instead of seeing how they fit into the big picture. Teams that don't really focus on caring for each other don't get very far. At some point, anything worth doing requires members of a team to need each other, count on each other, and help each other. Without team care, these teams will retreat at those moments. Team care starts with you.

Take a moment to consider these questions:

1. How will you care for the person you have a hard time connecting with?

2. How will you help your team members to really care about each other before their care for each other is ever tested?

89: COMMITMENT TO MISSION

I hate going to the gym in January. All year long, I have no problem going to the gym, but January is a nightmare. The track is overcrowded. There are people in line to use the weights, and there's a 30-minute limit on every machine. Getting a parking spot is even hard. Why? Because New Year's resolutions have started. The gym makes bank in January because of people who buy a yearlong membership but will be long gone by

February. In fact, by the last week of January, the gym is back to normal. Easy to park, no waiting, and not crowded.

People (let alone leaders) struggle with commitment. We all have good intentions. We all want the best in the end, but very few people actually get there. It's easy to dream, to set goals, to find amazing things to go after. But unless we follow through, all we did was dream.

Think about the things that will derail your commitment, and plan for them. Finals are coming, college visits are lingering in the future, homework will always pile up. So how will you be a leader that doesn't get derailed by circumstance, but stays committed to a mission?

Jesus tried so hard to teach this truth to his disciples. It wasn't going to be an easy road for them, and he knew it. He needed them to understand what their commitment would cost them and to plan for it. They would be persecuted, they would find themselves the outcasts, and most would even face martyrdom. But they were committed. They were ready. How is your commitment to Christ, to your team, to the mission?

90: SUPPORTIVE OF LEADERS

Probably the worst thing you can do to a cause, mission, a leader, or a brother/sister in Christ is to undermine them. When you are not in charge, it's easy to be divisive, even when you don't mean to. Sometimes you may disagree with a method, so you become a stick in the mud. Other times you may not give any effort. The problem with all this is that you are always leading. You are influencing others on the team, so when your actions look like they are undermining, you're deflating the team's potential. Even worse, when you undermine or become divisive, you will have bigger problems to deal with between you and God.

So be supportive. Swallow pride and go along with program. In the end it will spare a lot of people—including yourself—a lot of pain.

Let love and faithfulness never leave you; bind them around your neck, write them on the tablet of your heart. Then you will win favor and a good name in the sight of God and man (Proverbs 3:3-4).

91: CONSISTENT ACTIONS

When I'm the person in charge, I go overboard. I make sure that everything is set up and ready to go before a meeting or event. I arrive early to greet everyone and make sure no balls are dropped. I stay late to clean up and leave the place "better than when I got it." So why should that change just because my title does? You have a chance to truly serve your team and your leaders when you act like a real owner and someone who cares just as much as the leaders. Be faithful in the little things. Take serious the times when you don't receive the glory or get a special title, because you don't know what "big things" God is preparing you for.

92: SET OTHERS UP FOR SUCCESS

In my organization, we have several vans that our staff uses for mission trips or training events. Whenever someone is headed out the door, it seems like there are a million things to remember, from release forms to water coolers, so filling up the van with gas is often forgotten. This means that at 4 a.m. when one of us on the team is headed to the airport for an early flight, we're going to experience one of two things. Usually it's sigh/grunt as we realize someone left the van on empty but we don't have the time to get gas *and* make our flight. But occasionally, there's genuine relief when we realize our teammate filled it up for us. It wasn't their responsibility, but when they got back from whatever trip they were on, they took the time to fill it up for the next person.

Whether you are the leader or not, think about ways you can help your team. Navigate how you can set others up for success, not just for the mission, but for team unity and simply because you value them. Teams often love to serve outside of their walls, but great teams serve each other as well.

93: MAKE OTHERS HEROES

When a goal is scored in hockey, the first person celebrated is the person who scored it. The next person celebrated is the one who provided the assist. Records are kept, and the players' names are put into headlines. Everyone knows what they did, and people everywhere want to wear their jerseys and get their autographs. But what about the faithful defenseman who has rarely ever shot at the goal, but has made it possible for shots to be made? Or the guy who mostly sits on the bench but makes breakfast for his teammates and encourages them in countless ways whether they win or lose? Or even the parents that worked extra hours to pay for hockey gear and trainers all along?

There are more heroes in our midst than we know. But most of us are focused on how we can one day make it into the spotlight and get a little recognition for our own hard work. What if we stopped being all about us and took the time to bring the faithful, overlooked teammates to the front of the line? What if we recognized them and took the time for them? What if we even followed their example of sacrifice and commitment? There are a lot of unseen heroes on your team. Take the time to acknowledge them, to thank them, and to keep them motivated to bring greatness to the team.

CHAPTER II
HOW LEADERS FINISH

94: FINISH STRONG

I define finishing strong as doing what it takes, no matter the cost, to accomplish the goal. Finishing strong requires facing challenges, demonstrating courage, and doing things with excellence. Too many people start something with grand dreams and ideas, but either give up or wear out through the process. A leader must understand the power of sprinting past the finish line, rather than limping over it. Finishing strong encourages followers and builds respect. Leaders are men and women who don't just start things; they are people who finish strong.

95: DECIDE YOUR FINISH BEFORE YOU GET THERE

Have you ever set out on a journey without really knowing where you're going? Maybe it was a hike, a bike ride, or a road trip with friends. No doubt it can be fun to get out and explore, to find adventure, and to blaze a new trail. It's fun for a while, until you really get lost, you miss dinner, it starts getting dark, and you have no idea where you are. If you're starting a new project, building something, and guiding a team as a leader, you need to know what the finish line is. You need to define success before you start, and you need to communicate that to your followers. Leaders don't leave things up to chance.

96: MULTIPLICATION

We are called to lead, not because it brings fame or power, but because it brings Christ's message of salvation to the world. Great leaders understand they must build others into leaders, thus multiplying the impact of their leadership. God's kingdom moves forward because of leaders, and we must be diligent to pass our leadership on to others. You must lead beyond yourself. People who lead beyond themselves are more concerned with multiplying their leadership into others than they are with their personal achievement. Leading beyond yourself takes a commitment to the greater mission rather than to your own personal pride or desires. When you multiply your leadership into others, developing them into leaders, you propel the mission forward faster than if you hoard your leadership.

Take a moment to consider these questions:

1. Who are you getting ready to take over your role when you leave?

2. Who are you investing in?

97: EXCEEDING EXPECTATIONS

Great leaders are not willing to accept the status quo. They want more from themselves and from those around them. Teams that do great are willing to exceed expectations. Leaders who are afraid to work hard, put in extra effort, and dig deep to exceed expectations will have mediocre teams. But leaders who are willing to sacrifice and go above and beyond what is expected of them will have huge impact. When expectations begin to be exceeded, things get really fun. Goals begin to get met, the team feels successful, and new challenges and opportunities appear. Sometimes a leader needs to push a team to exceed expectations, because our natural tendency is to take the easy route. Be a leader that blows expectations out of the water, and encourage your team to do the same.

98: EXCELLENCE

If you were to peek under the hood of a Mercedes® with an AMG engine, you would find something that your car probably doesn't have: the builder's signature. Each AMG engine is built by one person from start to finish. It's a masterpiece that is held to incredibly high standards. Excellence is so important that the engine builder has to be willing to leave a signature on the engine. Think about that. If you're driving around and your car breaks down, you know exactly who is responsible, so that person had better make sure nothing is left undone. Every tiny detail will be held under their signature.

So what if we led like that? What if we were willing to sign our name over all our actions and words as a leader? Yes, ALL of them: the side conversations, the heart motivations, the shortcuts we took, the way we treated our teammates, and the words we used along the way. Are we really holding ourselves to a high standard and choosing the high road while serving our King?

99: LEAVING A LEGACY

Great leaders look beyond themselves, beyond the tasks of the day, beyond this present moment. They look to the future and gauge the impact of today on tomorrow. What's your legacy going to be? People are watching and learning from you as you lead. Your decisions have a much bigger impact than you probably realize. Leaders understand that legacy is much more about Jesus than it is about them. I want to be remembered as a leader who pointed people to Jesus Christ. I want to be known for other leaders I developed. I want to be a leader whose team achieved great things.

It's not about me; it's about HIM.

How do you want to be known and remembered? What kind of legacy will you leave?

SO RUN!

Leaders have no finish line. If we believe that we have been called to make a difference in people's lives, then we will be doing that to our last breath. Leaders need to understand that perseverance is one of their greatest tools. When you're going through failure or discouragement, remember that you are a child of the great King. When you experience victory and great joy, remember that you are a humble servant of the King. We persevere, not because we are great, but because we know the one who is great. Place your leadership in God's hands. Allow God to guide you, to give you wisdom, and to help you be creative. In God's hands we will do great things for God's glory, for God's purpose, and for God's name.

Therefore, strengthen your feeble arms and weak knees. "Make level paths for your feet," so that the lame may not be disabled, but rather healed" (Hebrews 12:12-13).